CHALLENGE ACCEPTED!

AN ACTIVITY BOOK FOR KIDS TO UNPLUG AND GET CREATIVE

CHALLENGE ACCEPTED!

AN ACTIVITY BOOK FOR KIDS TO UNPLUG AND GET CREATIVE

PARVEN KAUR

CORAL GABLES

For permission requests, please contact the publisher at:
Mango Publishing Group
2850 S Douglas Road, 2nd Floor
Coral Gables, FL 33134 USA
info@mango.bz

For special orders, quantity sales, course adoptions and corporate sales, please email the publisher at sales@mango.bz. For trade and wholesale sales, please contact Ingram Publisher Services at customer.service@ingramcontent.com or +1.800.509.4887.

Challenge Accepted!: An Activity Book for Kids to Unplug and Get Creative

ISBN: (print) 978-1-64250-620-4 (ebook) 978-1-64250-621-1
BISAC category code

Printed in the United States of America

For my loving and supporting family; especially
my darling girls—You are my inspiration.

THIS JOURNAL BELONGS TO

_____

IF YOU COULD CHOOSE ANOTHER
NAME, WHAT WOULD IT BE?

_____

WRITE YOUR NAME BACKWARDS:

_____

WRITE YOUR NAME IN A FANCY WAY:

⚠ Warning!

While completing the challenges, you may get messy and dirty. You may get covered in paint, tape, and glue. Don't be afraid to embrace the fun of making mistakes and be as wacky as possible!

HOW TO USE THIS BOOK

1. Follow the instructions on each page and don't be afraid to get messy!

2. You can work on any page you feel like first—there is no order to the fun.

3. You can ask a friend or a family member to help you complete any of the challenges.

Date I started this book:

_____

Where I am:

_____

What I am wearing:

_____

What the weather is like:

_____

8

Fun supplies to have:

Anything you can use for drawing, writing, cutting and sticking. Color pencils, glue, tape and scissors.

You will need more of this

Fun, imagination, creativity, bravery, stuff for recycling (trash) and, most importantly, an open-mindedness and willingness to try new things!

MY FIRST...

Vacation

School

Friend

Pet

Teacher

YOU'RE AN ARTIST!

Make your own cover for this
book. Give it a new name.

TREE OF HOPE

Fill in the leaves with things you are grateful for. Color the tree.

FILL IN THE CIRCLES WITH ALL THE DIFFERENT EMOJIS YOU CAN THINK OF.

Color the emojis based on their moods.

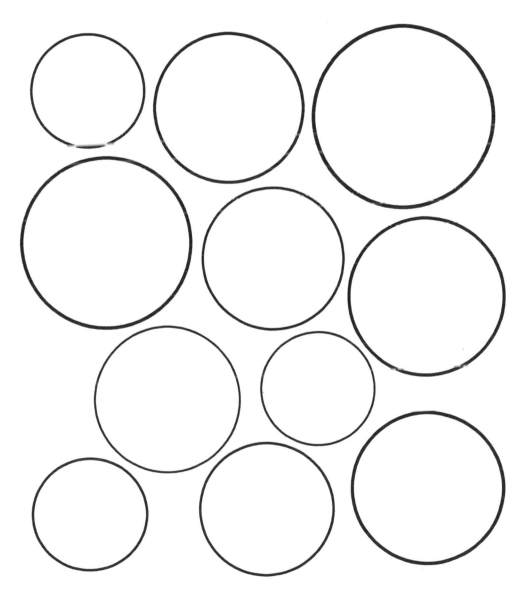

REMEMBER THE POSITION OF THE STARS, THEN CLOSE YOUR EYES AND CONNECT THEM.

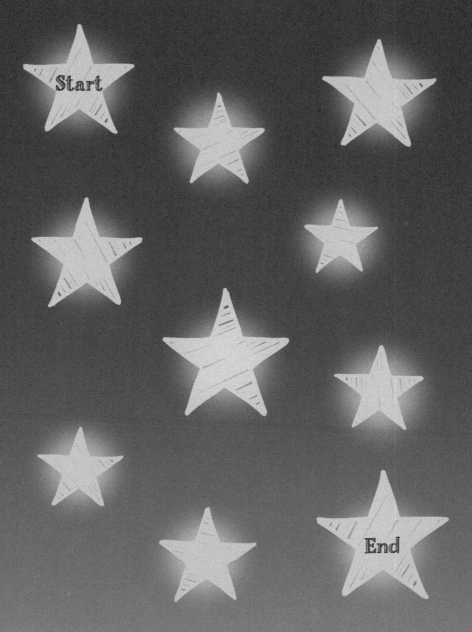

I AM UNIQUE.

Fill in this fingerprint with all the
things that make you unique.

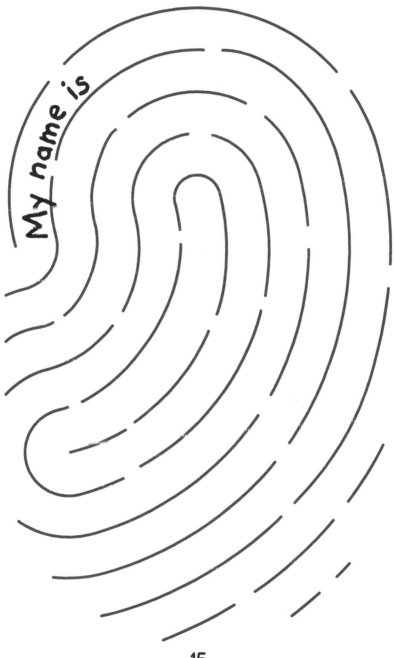

My name is

DRAW A MAP FROM HOME TO SCHOOL.

Be as detailed as you can using
the landmarks from the next page,
you can draw your own too.

CUT OUT THESE PICTURES TO HELP WITH YOUR MAP.

MY ONE-YEAR BUCKET LIST

A bucket list is a list of things you want
to do in your life. Write all the things
you want to do in the next year.

COLLECT SOME LEAVES, PAINT THEM, AND STAMP THEM ON THIS PAGE.

DRAW A MAP OF YOUR NEIGHBORHOOD.

MY SIGNATURE

Get your mom and dad to pop their
signatures on this page, then create your own.
Write as many signatures as you can think of.

_____   _____

          Mom   Dad

My Test Signatures

Circle **3** signatures you like best
and then ask **10** people to vote for
which is the best signature.

_____

_____

_____

_____

_____

Voted Best Signature:

_____

THE JAR OF SELF-LOVE

Fill this jar with things you love about yourself.
Decorate the rest of the jar with glitter.

TORNADO IN A BOTTLE

Create your own tornado in a bottle!

Supplies:

- Two 2-liter bottles
- Duct tape
- Water
- Dish soap
- Glitter (optional)

How to make tornado in a bottle:

1. Fill one 2-liter bottle ¾ of the way full with water.

2. Add a squirt of dish soap and a sprinkle of glitter.

3. Take the empty water bottle and put it on top of the filled one, opening to opening.

4. Tape the bottles together so no water can escape.

5. Turn the bottles over and swirl the top bottle in a circle a few times.

6. Now watch a tornado appear!

DRAW SOMETHING FUN ON THIS PORTRAIT.

For example, add a moustache, hat, tie, etc.

MY FAVORITE FOODS

Find wrappers of your favorite
foods and stick them here.

DRAW YOURSELF AS A SUPER HERO.

Create a drawing of yourself as a super hero. Think about what suit you'd like to have and which super powers.

DRAW YOURSELF AS A VILLAIN.

Be as bad and scary as possible...muhahaha!

FORTUNE COOKIE

Ask your friends or family members to make a wish for you and fill the fortune cookies below. Open this page in a few months to see if their wishes came true.

Tear this page out. Follow the
instructions on the next page to
create your own paper airplane!

BUILD AN AIRPLANE

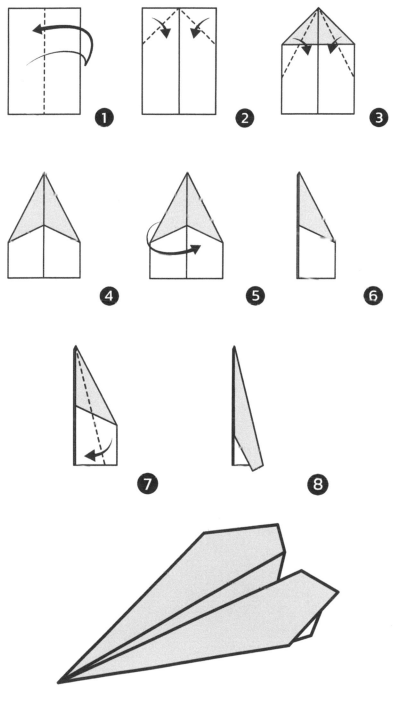

FLYING SCHOOL

Follow these instructions to create
your own paper airplane game!

1. Tear the next page out and cut out the
   circle in the middle of the page.

2. Ask a friend or a family member to hold
   the paper up.

3. Fly your airplane through it! You can play
   a game to see who gets it through the
   circle the most.

Fly thru here!

CUT THIS OUT

DESIGN YOUR OWN T-SHIRT

Decorate as many shirts as you want!

Write down all the slogans you will put on your T-shirts.

ROLL THE DICE

Cut this out and roll the figure into
a dice. Whichever prompt you
get first, complete that task!

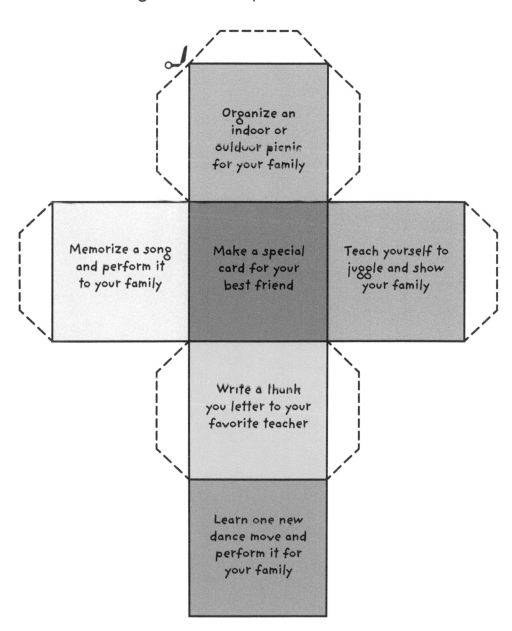

Organize an indoor or outdoor picnic for your family

Memorize a song and perform it to your family

Make a special card for your best friend

Teach yourself to juggle and show your family

Write a thank you letter to your favorite teacher

Learn one new dance move and perform it for your family

Use paint,

magic markers,

or glitter to brighten up

the night sky on

the next page.

LOVE IT OR HATE IT

Color the heart below in **red** for things you love, **black** for things you hate and green if you are unsure how you feel about it.

Scary movies

Christmas

Insects

Spicy food

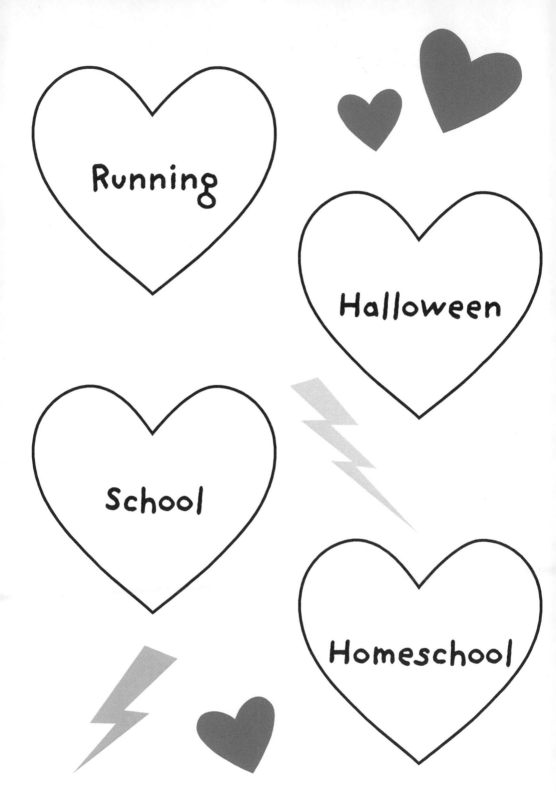

Running

Halloween

School

Homeschool

IF YOU HAD A BOX OF COURAGE, WHAT WOULD YOU FIND IN IT?

Write down all the things you want
to do but are too scared to try.

MY LITTLE PUPPY

Tear the next page out and
follow the instructions to create
your own puppy origami.

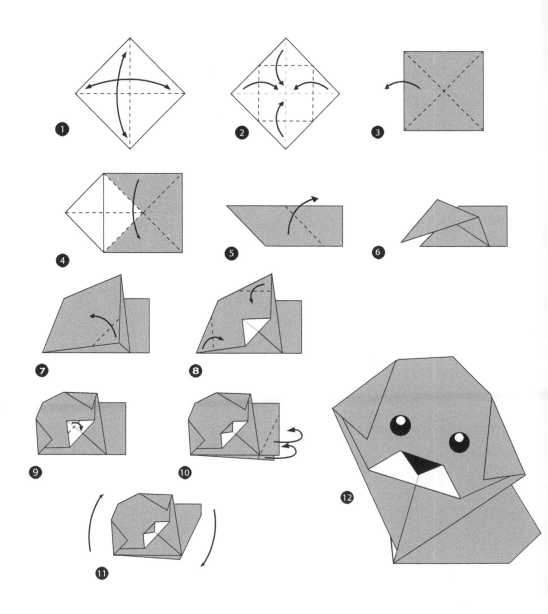

CREATE A NEW CHARACTER FOR YOUR FAVORITE CARTOON OR MOVIE.

THIS IS: _____

WHO IS FROM THE MOVIE/CARTOON:

_____

WHO CAN: _____

_____

AND IS A GREAT ADDITION TO THE MOVIE/CARTOON BECAUSE:

_____

_____

AND IS LIKED BY EVERYONE BECAUSE:

_____

_____

_____

DRAW WHAT THE NEW CHARACTER LOOKS LIKE:

FILL IN THIS PAGE WITH STAMPS OR STICKERS.

Draw the images in the previous page here
using the hand you don't usually write with.

COLOR EACH TRIANGLE
WITH A DIFFERENT COLOR.

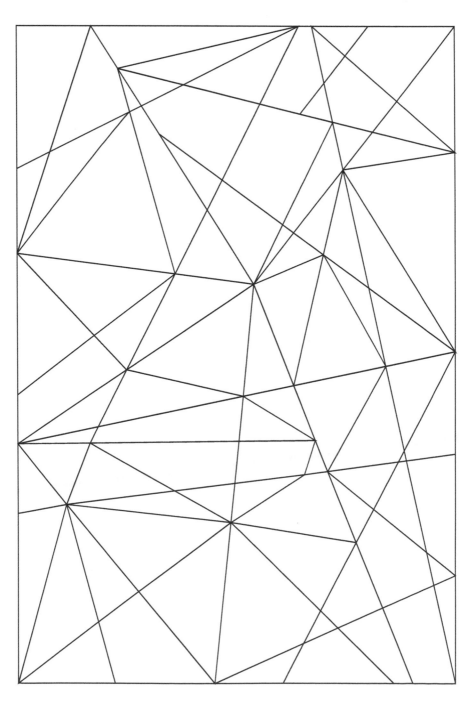

CREATE YOUR OWN MONEY

Imagine you run your own country
and have been given the responsibility
to create a new currency.

What is the currency called?

_____

Draw what the money would look like:

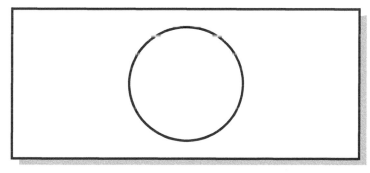

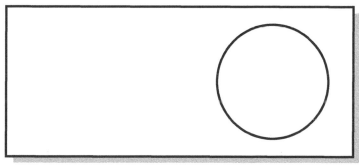

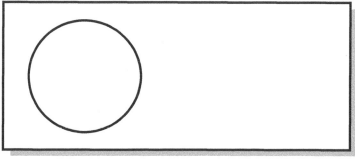

Draw what the coins would look like.

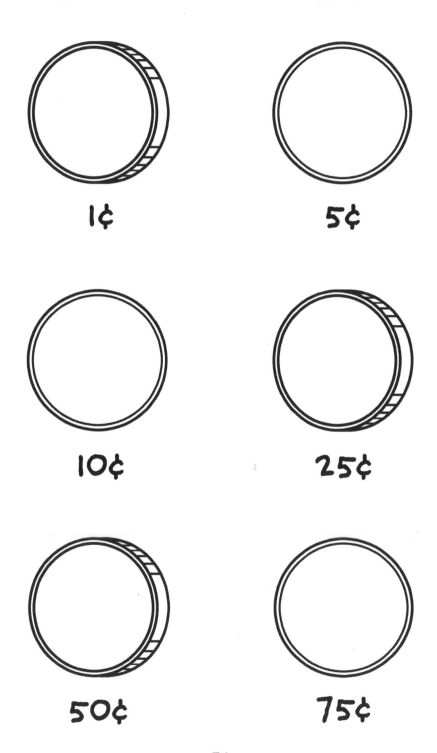

1¢

5¢

10¢

25¢

50¢

75¢

DREAM BOARD

A dream board represents something you want to accomplish.

Create your own dream board on the next page. Feel free to include pictures, drawings, and words that make you smile.

Something I want to accomplish this year

Hopes and Dreams

Something I love about myself

Books I want to read

Places I
want to go

59

CREATE YOUR OWN PLANET!

Name:_____

Temperature:_____

How big (miles):_____

Number of inhabitants:_____

Fun facts about the planet:_____

_____

Natural resources in the planet:_____

_____

Create 5 laws all citizens of the planet
must follow:

1. _____

2. _____

3. _____

4. _____

5. _____

Draw what your planet would look like!

Pick a number

between 63 to 90.

Go to that page.

Go forward 5 pages

(if you can't then go
backward 5 pages).

Complete the challenge on

that page NOW.

DESIGN THESE SQUARES INTO ANYTHING THAT YOU CHOOSE IN LESS THAN THREE MINUTES.

WORDS, WORDS, WORDS

Open a random book to any page. Close your eyes and place your finger onto the page. Whatever word you finger lands on, write as much as you can about that word until the box is full. Just write whatever that comes to mind, even if it doesn't make sense.

When you finish the first box, find another random word for the next few boxes.

Word: _____

_____

_____

Word: _____

_____

_____

_____

Word: _____

_____

_____

_____

TIME TRAVEL

This is a time travel machine. Think of a place or moment you would like to revisit.

Enter where and when:

Why do you want to go back there?

Who was there with you?

What were you doing there?

Circle what the weather was like that day:

AWARD NOMINATIONS

Write down the name of the person most likely to win an award in the categories below. Tear this page and give that person the award below.

Become a Millionare

Finish a marathon

Getting locked in the bathroom

Complete an impossible misison

MORSE CODE

Did you know that people used to communicate using codes like the one below before we had telephones?

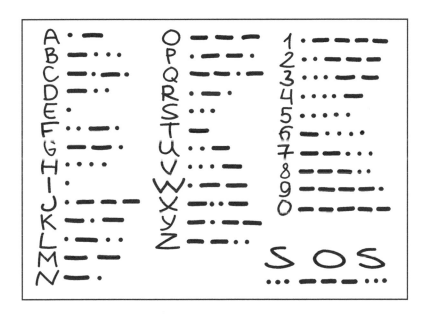

Write your name in Morse Code:

_____

Can you decode this Morse? Ask a friend or a family member to help if you are stuck

. / .-.. --- ...- . / -.-- --- ..-

_____

ASK A FRIEND OR A FAMILY MEMBER TO FILL IN THIS PAGE.

I like the owner of this book because:

_____

_____

_____

Funniest thing the owner of this book has said:

_____

_____

_____

What do you see the owner of this book
doing 10 years from now?

_____

_____

_____

3 words to describe the owner of this book:

_____

FOOT DAY

Measure the length of your family's feet. You can use a ruler or whatever you'd like! For example, a banana, TV remote, or your fingers. (Example: My dad's foot is 1½ bananas long.)

Name:_____

Length of left foot:_____

Name:_____

Length of right foot:_____

Name:_____

Length of right foot plus left:_____

Name:_____

Length of right foot plus left divided by 2:

_____

Total number of toes at home:_____

71

THE GREAT OUTDOORS

Take this book outside.

Draw the first thing you can **hear**
(example: a bird, car, or dog).

Draw the first **red** object you see.

Draw the first thing you can **smell**.

Draw something (or someone)
that is **taller than you**.

Draw the first thing you thing
you see that is **moving**.

Draw the first **fluffy** thing you see.

BATTLE OF THE BALANCE

Gather a group of people and get each person to balance this book on their head while standing on one leg. If this gets too easy, stand on your tippy toe! Use a timer to see how long each person lasts.

The player who lasts the longest wins!

Player 1:_____
Time:_____

Player 2:_____
Time:_____

Player 3:_____
Time:_____

Player 4:_____
Time:_____

My time:_____

And the winner is:_____

Balance Champion

WHY IS HE GRUMPY?

Finish the drawing on this page then write
a story about it on the next page.

The story of the grumpy man:

_____

_____

_____

_____

_____

_____

_____

_____

_____

_____

_____

_____

_____

_____

_____

_____

_____

PLAN YOUR DREAM VACATION

Where would you go?

_____

How long would you stay there?

_____

Who would you go with?

_____

List 5 things you would do there:

_____

What would the season be like?

_____

What would you pack in your suit case?

_____

Where would you stay?

_____

What souvenirs would you bring home?

_____

NEWSPAPER QUEST

Collect old newspapers or magazines for two weeks. Then go through them and find pictures of transportation (cars, buses, trains, airplanes, or boats). Cut them out and stick your favorites here!

YOUR VICTORIES

It is great to celebrate the small things that you have achieved this week. It could be making your bed, waking up on time, doing your homework, etc. Fill in the medals below with your victories. Just because it is small does not mean it is not important.

CREATE YOUR OWN RESTAURANT

Imagine opening up your own restaurant. What would it be like?

NAME:_____

LOCATION:_____

WHAT KIND OF FOOD:_____

NUMBER OF WORKERS:_____

OPENING HOURS:_____

Write the name of your restaurant
in the banner below.

Brainstorm some logos for your restaurant.

Create a menu for your restaurant.

MENU

Appetizers

_____

_____

_____

Mains

_____

_____

_____

Desserts

_____

_____

_____

Drinks

_____

_____

_____

DRAW 10 OBJECTS THAT COME TO MIND WHEN YOU THINK OF YOUR BEDROOM.

FINISH THE STORY

Once upon a time...

There was a:

 Dragon   Princess   ☐ Prince

Named:_____

Who lived in a:

☐ Cave   Castle   Mountain

One day while walking…

_____

_____

_____

_____

_____

_____

_____

_____

And then…

_____

_____

_____

_____

_____

_____

_____

_____

There was a:

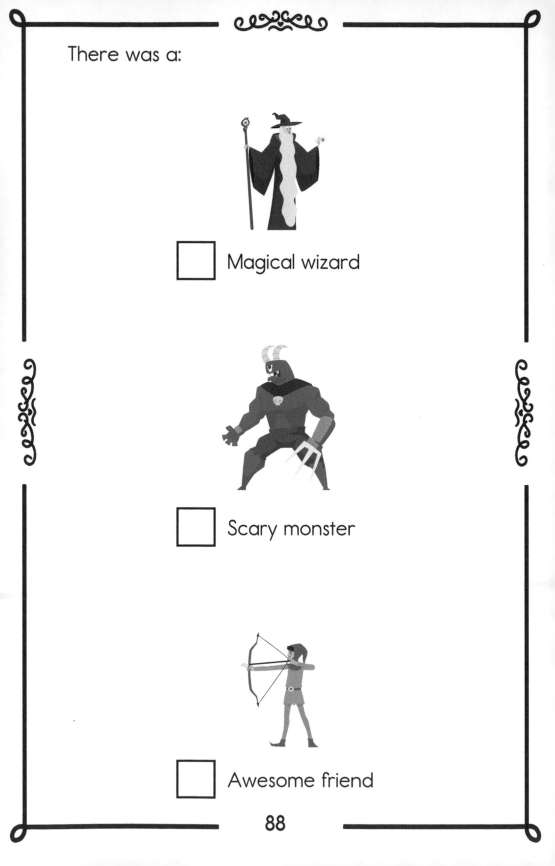

☐ Magical wizard

☐ Scary monster

☐ Awesome friend

Unfortunately…

_____

_____

_____

_____

_____

_____

But luckily…

_____

_____

_____

_____

_____

_____

And they lived happily ever after.

The End

DRAW THE IMAGE BELOW WITH BOTH HANDS AT THE SAME TIME. FEEL FREE TO DECORATE THE PAGE AFTER!

CREATE YOUR OWN SCHOOL

Name of school:

_____

Number of students:_____

Number of teachers:_____

What you would study:

_____

School start and end time:_____

Length of recess break:_____

Extra-curricular activities:

_____

_____

_____

Draw a special uniform for your school.

What would your school schedule look like?

MON				
TUES				
WED				
THURS				
FRI				

93

A WALK IN A MAGICAL FOREST

Complete the story!

Imagine you are in the forest...

You suddenly hear:

□ A bear roaring   □ Someone running

□ Leaves rustling   □ The sound of a waterfall

You followed the sound and found:

_____

_____

_____

_____

_____

It made you feel:

☐ Happy

☐ Scared

☐ Sad

☐ Nervous

Just at that moment, you heard someone call out your name. You turned around and saw:

☐ A superhero (you can name him or her):

_____

☐ Your best friend

☐ A zombie

Unfortunately…

_____

_____

_____

_____

_____

_____

But luckily…

_____

_____

_____

_____

_____

**And you went back home feeling
happy and safe.**

The End

DON'T WASTE IT

Collect unused stationery and stick it onto this page. For example, Post-it notes, paper clips, left over erasers, etc. Create an artistic masterpiece!

SECRET IDENTITY

Imagine being a secret agent. Create a new identity for yourself. Fill this page in a different language if possible.

Agent name:_____

_____

Place of birth:_____

_____

Clearance level:_____

_____

Agent start date:_____

_____

Special talents:___ _____

_____

What is your secret mission?

_____

_____

_____

AGENT'S FINGER PRINT ID

Dip each finger in paint or ink
and stamp it below.

THUMB

INDEX

MIDDLE

RING

CONFIDENTIAL

PINKY

SCAVENGER HUNT

Go on an outdoor scavenger hunt. Tick
the boxes on what you were able to find.

☐ Ants   ☐ Butterflies   ☐ Pinecones

☐ Ladybug   ☐ Yellow flowers   ☐ Clouds

☐ Rocks   ☐ Sticks   ☐ Feathers

☐ Trees   ☐ Birds

BUILD SOMETHING

Look through the recycling bin and find **10** things you can use to build something with. For example: build the tallest tower in your home, a robot, or anything you fancy!

List the things you found:

1._____

2._____

3._____

4._____

5._____

6._____

7._____

8._____

9._____

10._____

Draw or describe what you built.

MY SECRET MESSAGE

Write down a secret message to yourself and place it in the envelope on the next page.

Tear this page out. Follow the outlines on the next page to fold it into an envelope.

HOW TO MAKE AN ENVELOPE

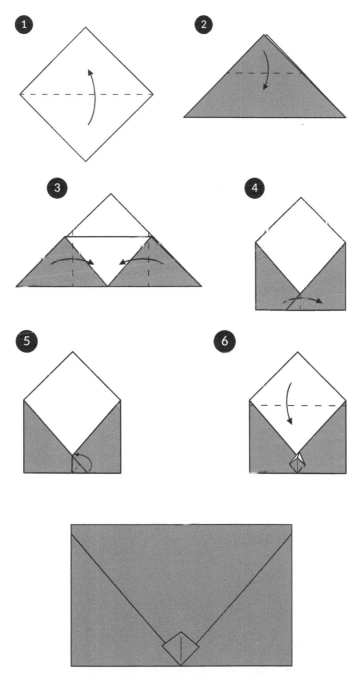

SAY SOMETHING NICE TO THE WORLD!

THE CANDY EXPERIMENT

Get **three** pieces of hard candy, such as candy canes. Place each candy in a different cup of liquid...

Cup 1: Cool water

I predict that the candy will:_____

_____

What actually happened:_____

_____

Cup 2: Hot water

I predict that the candy will:_____

_____

What actually happened:_____

_____

Cup 3: Vinegar

I predict that the candy will:_____

_____

What actually happened:_____

_____

CREATE YOUR OWN HAUNTED HOUSE

Where would it be?

_____

How many rooms would it have?_____

What are the spooky things found inside the house?

_____

_____

_____

Who lives inside the house?

_____

_____

_____

What creepy sounds would you hear?

_____

_____

_____

Draw what it would look like.

FOOTIE

Trace these dotted lines as best as you can...using the pencil with your foot!

POSITIVE THOUGHTS

Write as many affirmations as
you can think of here.

I am awesome

MY PERFECT PIZZA

Draw toppings that should be
added to this pizza.

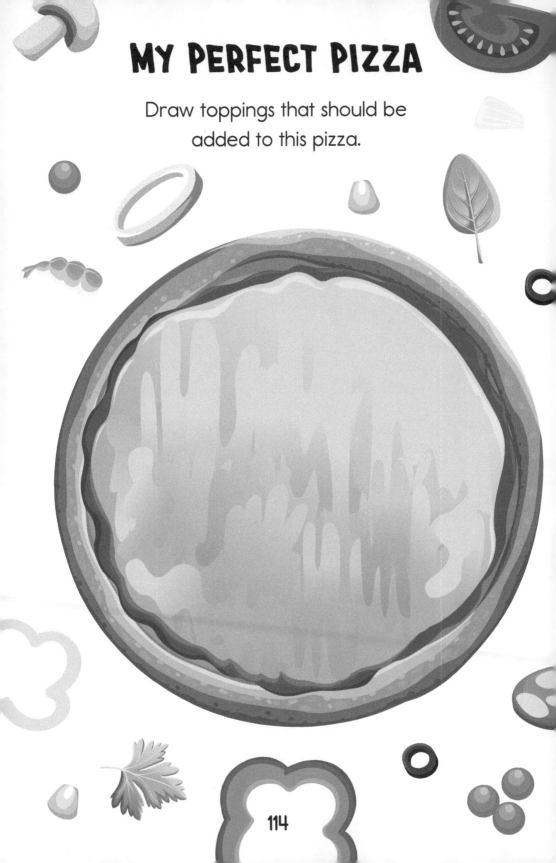

114

SPLATTER TIME

Create your own "bubble paint"!

Supplies:

- Paper
- 3 empty cups
- Liquid soap
- Food coloring
- A straw

How to create your own bubble paint:

1. Fill each cup with liquid soap.

2. Fill each of those cups with different paint color.

3. Blow bubbles into each cup using a straw.

4. Get the piece of paper and swipe it across the cup.

5. Pop the bubbles on the paper with your hands.

6. Once the paper is dried, stick it to this page.

MAKE A MESS HERE!

1. Collect things that are only found outdoors.

2. Add some glue to this page and rub this paper with sand or soil

3. Stick the things you found on the paper using glue or tape.

4. When the paper has dried, feel free to add some drawings or clippings of other things you like outdoors!

INSPIRING WORD CLOUD

Browse through newspapers, coupons, and magazines and cut out words that make you feel happy. For example: food, sun, birds, etc.

FOUR SEASONS

In the space below, stick things you like most about each season. Otherwise draw things that you like best about each season.

Summer	Autumn
Winter	Spring

JOURNAL BASKETBALL

1. Tear out this page.

2. Crumple it into a ball.

3. Have this journal standing.

4. Throw the paper and see if you can get the journal to drop.

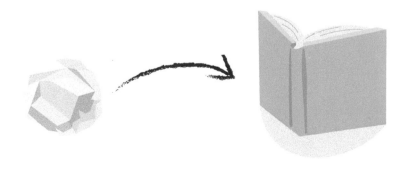

YOU ARE ALMOST AT THE END OF THIS CHALLENGE!

Draw how this book made you feel:

Congratulations! You have successfully completed this book.

Completion date:_____

How many days it took to complete the book:

_____

How many hours it took to complete the book:

_____

Reward yourself with the crown on the next page. Decorate it, cut it out, and put it on your head for the day!

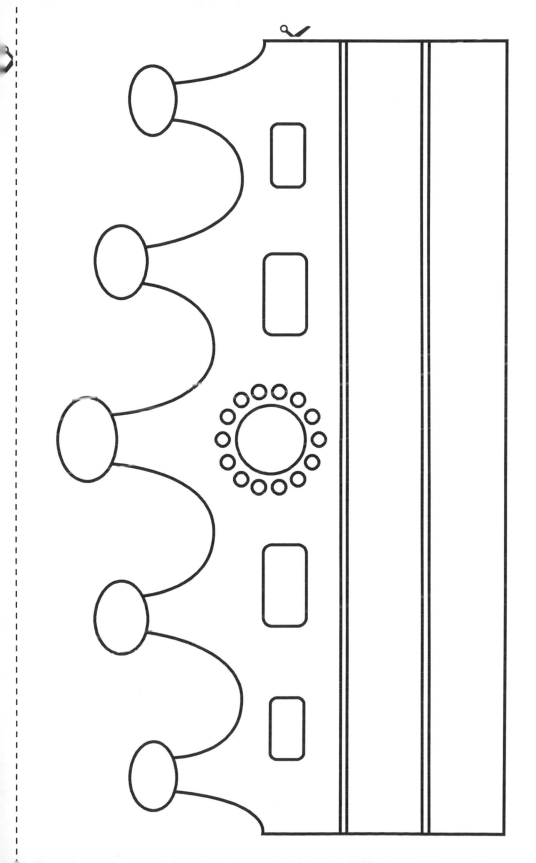

NOW CHALLENGE A FRIEND TO FINISH THIS BOOK FASTER THAN YOU DID.

I
WOULD LIKE TO
CHALLENGE:

_____

About the Author

Parven Kaur is the founder of *Kids N Clicks*, a web resource that help parents and children thrive in a digital world.

After graduating with an MSc in corporate governance from the London School of Economics and Political Science, she worked in the corporate sector before moving into digital media consultancy.

She has extensive experience in the digital / social media arena and has been a consultant for various charitable organisations across Scotland. She was recognised as a "Digital Pioneer" by the Scottish Council for Voluntary Organisations for her work with a women's charity in the east of Scotland.

Following her foray into digital parenting, she was appointed as an Ambassador for the Parenting 2.0 organization for improving digital literacy. She blogged for Common Sense Media, Family Online Safety Institute, and many other international organizations. She is also an expert contributor in digital parenting by Internet Matters and has been featured in *The Telegraph* in the UK.

Parven lives with her family in Edinburgh and actively contributes to digital parenting news and tips on Facebook, Clubhouse, Pinterest as well as on her *Kids N Clicks* website and blog. She spends the rest of her time with her little toddler, enjoying long walks in the Scottish countryside.

DragonFruit, an imprint of Mango Publishing, publishes high-quality children's books to inspire a love of lifelong learning in readers. DragonFruit publishes a variety of titles for kids, including children's picture books, nonfiction series, toddler activity books, pre-K activity books, science and education titles, and ABC books. Beautiful and engaging, our books celebrate diversity, spark curiosity, and capture the imaginations of parents and children alike.

Mango Publishing, established in 2014, publishes an eclectic list of books by diverse authors. We were named the Fastest Growing Independent Publisher by Publishers Weekly in 2019 and 2020. Our success is bolstered by our main goal, which is to publish high-quality books that will make a positive impact in people's lives.

Our readers are our most important resource; we value your input, suggestions, and ideas. We'd love to hear from you—after all, we are publishing books for you!

Please stay in touch with us and follow us at:

Instagram: @dragonfruitkids
Facebook: Mango Publishing
Twitter: @MangoPublishing
LinkedIn: Mango Publishing
Pinterest: Mango Publishing

Sign up for our newsletter at www.mangopublishinggroup.com and receive a free book! Join us on Mango's journey to change publishing, one book at a time.

CPSIA information can be obtained
at www.ICGtesting.com
Printed in the USA
JSHW010957140521
14733JS00003B/4

9 781642 506204